THE HANDLESS MAIDEN

THE HANDLESS
MAIDEN

Vicki Feaver

CAPE POETRY

First published 1994

1 3 5 7 9 10 8 6 4 2

© Vicki Feaver 1994

Vicki Feaver has asserted her right
under the Copyright, Designs and Patents Act, 1988
to be identified as the author of this work

First published in the United Kingdom in 1994 by
Jonathan Cape
Random House, 20 Vauxhall Bridge Road, London SW1V 2SA

Random House Australia (Pty) Limited
20 Alfred Street, Milsons Point, Sydney,
New South Wales 2061, Australia

Random House New Zealand Limited
18 Poland Road, Glenfield,
Auckland 10, New Zealand

Random House South Africa (Pty) Limited
PO Box 337, Bergvlei, South Africa

Random House UK Limited Reg. No. 954009

A CIP catalogue record for this book
is available from the British Library

ISBN 0 224 03892 3

Typeset in Bembo by
SX Composing Ltd, Rayleigh, Essex
Printed and bound in Great Britain
by Mackays of Chatham PLC

FOR MY DAUGHTERS —
JANE, EMILY AND JESSICA

ACKNOWLEDGEMENTS

I would like to thank the editors of the magazines and anthologies in which some of these poems first appeared: *Ambit, Independent on Sunday, London Magazine, London Review of Books, New Statesman, New Welsh Review, Observer, Poetry Book Society Anthology 1989* and *1991, Slow Dancer, Spectator, Sunday Times, Times Literary Supplement, With a Poet's Eye* (ed. Pat Adams, 1986).

'Teddy Bears' won a prize in the National Poetry Competition in 1981. 'Lily Pond' won a prize in the Arvon Competition in 1992. 'Judith' won a Forward Prize in 1993.

I would also like to thank the Administrators of Hawthornden Castle for awarding me a Hawthornden Fellowship in 1993 and The West Sussex Institute for allowing me to take it up.

I also want to thank Bernard Loughlin who let me stay at Annaghmakerrig in 1991 and 1992.

CONTENTS

MARIGOLDS

Not the flowers men give women –
delicately-scented freesias,
stiff red roses, carnations
the shades of bridesmaids' dresses,
almost sapless flowers,
drying and fading – but flowers
that wilt as soon as their stems
are cut, leaves blackening
as if blighted by the enzymes
in our breath, rotting to a slime
we have to scour from the rims
of vases; flowers that burst
from tight, explosive buds, rayed
like the sun, that lit the path
up the Thracian mountain, that we wound
into our hair, stamped on
in ecstatic dance, that remind us
we are killers, can tear the heads
off men's shoulders;
flowers we still bring
secretly and shamefully
into the house, stroking
our arms and breasts and legs
with their hot orange fringes,
the smell of arousal.

CIRCE

'No one had a heart more susceptible to love'
Ovid, *Metamorphoses*, XIV

Because he wouldn't enter me
I made her unenterable – Scylla,
the nymph who fled from the god
whose spawn and thrashing fish tail
I wanted. I spilled my powders
into the pool where she waded
to cool herself in the gauzy
noon heat – stayed to see her crotch
grow teeth, to watch her run
from her own legs.

My father is the fiery sun.
Why do I fall for cold men?
Picus, so beautiful
on his lathered horse
I couldn't move for burning.
I covered the moon, the stars,
even my father's furnace face
with the wet sponges of clouds,
conjured a boar from the air
for him to hunt, caught up with him
in a thicket, both of us gasping.
I thought he'd lick the sweat
from my small brown breasts
like the men in Venus's stories.
When I saw he was ready for flight
I gave him feathers.

I frighten men. Even Ulysses
I had to bargain with: a year in my bed
to set his friends upright again,
unglue their trotters.
I stretched nights into weeks –
lived in the damp, ripe, gooseberry rot
of my sheets, feeding my wanderer warrior
on jellies and syrups
to help him keep up with a goddess.
In the end, it was me who sent him away.
It made me too sad: hearing
my name on his tongue
like the hiss of a tide withdrawing.

BEAUTY AND THE BEAST

He'd eat her eventually,
when he got tired
of watching her eat:

tucking the white napkin
into the top of her blouse,
picking the flesh

off a peacock's leg
with delicate teeth,
or with her tongue

sucking a clam
from its saucer shell.
After a few nights

he couldn't face
trotting to the fields
to pounce on a sheep.

While the pearl buttons
flew off her dresses,
his belly drooped

like an empty bag,
his fangs hung loose
in shrinking gums.

He sent her home to her father.
He knew he'd die
if he didn't eat raw meat.

On the day she came back
he lay in the long grass
of the rose garden,

eyes closed, meaning
to feast on her liver.
He heard her step, tasted

something wet and salt
on his lips, sensed hands
unzipping his furry pelt.

WOOD-PIGEONS

The army chap says –
to get conversation flowing –
'Women are more adapted to life
than men. They get less hurt.
Keep more of themselves back.'

His wife of thirty years,
a bony, brainy woman
with pale, frizzy curls and
baby-blue eyes, gently remonstrates.
The others join in –

chuckling, smoothing,
while trying to wrestle
with small tough parcels
that sit in red pools of sauce
on each blue-patterned plate.

In the end, the hostess
has to raid the kitchen drawer
for the sharpest knives
so her guests can dismember
the wood-pigeons.

In her silver-beaded dress
she looks like the knife-thrower's girl
at the circus – carvers
bunched in her hands
like dangerous flowers.

NAKED GIRL WITH EGG

after Lucian Freud

While she discards coat, skirt,
cashmere sweater, a string of pearls,
and lies ready on the bed, left hand
propping her left breast, body twisted
in an S, he fries two eggs

and brings them in on a white dish.
Then he sets to work – his brush
slithering over lustrous flesh,
the coarse dark hair between her legs,
like a tongue seeking salt.

She keeps her mind fixed on the eggs,
as if by concentrating hard enough
she'll discover a meaning as obvious
as in one of those paintings
where a skull, bottom left, equals death.

What could be homelier, or more comforting,
than to dip toast soldiers
into soft yellow yolks? Yet she thinks
of a day on the moors when she trod
on a curlew's nest, and of herself

posed on the black coverlet
to satisfy something – still loose
in the world – that likes nothing better
than to be fed on a naked girl
with two fried eggs.

OI YOI YOI

for Roger Hilton

The lady has no shame.
Wearing not a stitch
she is lolloping across
an abstract beach
towards a notional sea.

I like the whisker of hair
under her armpit. It suggests
that she's not one of those women
who are always trying to get rid
of their smell.

You were more interested
in her swinging baroque tits
and the space between her thighs
than the expression on her face.
That you've left blank.

But her *mons veneris*
you've etched in black ink
with the exuberance of a young lad
caught short on a bellyful of beer
scrawling on a wall in the Gents.

As a woman I ought to object.
But she looks happy enough.
And which of us doesn't occasionally
want one of the old gods to come down
and chase us over the sands?

doesn't know why he's such a strong swimmer;
why he drinks nothing but frothy black Guinness;
why when he stands at the top
of a long flight of stairs
he has to struggle to stop himself
raising his arms, diving into a pool
of swaying air; why in his fantasies
the girls undress – uncovering white necks
and shoulders, brown and pink-nippled breasts,
the dark nests between their legs –
among reeds, under the grey-yellow light
of willows; why the women – in bars,
airports, at the Tennis and Squash Club –
he never spends more than a night with
seem flaky, juiceless; why he wants to smear
their mouths and ears and stomachs
with slime; why the water he shakes
from his hair, that twists
off his shoulders in the shower,
glitters with sticklebacks, snails,
minnows; why his wife follows
his wet footprints with a cloth;
makes him wear slippers.

IRONING

I used to iron everything:
my iron flying over sheets and towels
like a sledge chased by wolves over snow,

the flex twisting and crinking
until the sheath frayed, exposing
wires like nerves. I stood like a horse

with a smoking hoof
inviting anyone who dared
to lie on my silver-padded board,

to be pressed to the thinness
of dolls cut from paper.
I'd have commandeered a crane

if I could, got the welders at Jarrow
to heat me an iron the size of a tug
to flatten the house.

Then for years I ironed nothing.
I put the iron in a high cupboard.
I converted to crumpledness.

And now I iron again: shaking
dark spots of water onto wrinkled
silk, nosing into sleeves, round

buttons, breathing the sweet heated smell
hot metal draws from newly-washed
cloth, until my blouse dries

to a shining, creaseless blue,
an airy shape with room to push
my arms, breasts, lungs, heart into.

THE HANDLESS MAIDEN[*]

When all the water had run from her mouth,
and I'd rubbed her arms and legs,
and chest and belly and back,
with clumps of dried moss;
and I'd put her to sleep in a nest of grass,
and spread her dripping clothes on a bush,
and held her again – her heat passing
into my breast and shoulder,
the breath I couldn't believe in
like a tickling feather on my neck,
I let myself cry. I cried for my hands
my father cut off; for the lumpy, itching scars
of my stumps; for the silver hands –
my husband gave me – that spun and wove
but had no feeling; and for my handless arms
that let my baby drop – unwinding
from the tight swaddling cloth
as I drank from the brimming river.
And I cried for my hands that sprouted
in the red-orange mud – the hands
that write this, grasping
her curled fists.

---

* *In Grimm's version of this story the woman's hands grow back
because she's good for seven years. But in a Russian version they
grow as she plunges her arms into a river to save her drowning
baby.*

CRAB APPLE JELLY

Every year you said it wasn't worth the trouble –
you'd better things to do with your time –
and it made you furious when the jars
were sold at the church fête
for less than the cost of the sugar.

And every year you drove into the lanes
around Calverton to search
for the wild trees whose apples
looked as red and as sweet as cherries,
and tasted sourer than gooseberries.

You cooked them in the wide copper pan
Grandma brought with her from Wigan,
smashing them against the sides
with a long wooden spoon to split
the skins, straining the pulp

through an old muslin nappy.
It hung for days, tied with string
to the kitchen steps, dripping
into a bowl on the floor –
brown-stained, horrible,

a head in a bag, a pouch
of sourness, of all that went wrong
in that house of women. The last drops
you wrung out with your hands;
then, closing doors and windows

to shut out the clamouring wasps,
you boiled up the juice with sugar,
dribbling the syrup onto a cold plate
until it set to a glaze,
filling the heated jars.

When the jars were cool
you held one up to the light
to see if the jelly had cleared.
Oh Mummy, it was as clear and shining
as stained glass and the colour of fire.

DAWLISH, 1947

In the kitchen, Aunt Inge,
who in the war was accused
of hanging nappies on the line
to send messages to the Germans
and who, the first Christmas

in Devon, cut and bundled
and sent up to London
enough mistletoe and holly
to almost pay for this house
with its crumbling stone terrace

overlooking the sea – 'Some people
always land on their feet!' –
stands with two bantams
squawking and fluttering
in her podgy red hands.

I am crying. It's the heat
and excitement, my mother says,
dabbing cotton wool soaked
in cold pink calamine lotion
onto my burning back.

On the terrace,
the little cousin is calling:
'*Schmetterling! Schmetterling!*'
'It's not! It's not!' I scream.
'It's a butterfly!'

WASPS

If you don't hurt them
they won't hurt you,
my father told me.

But I didn't believe him,
or that he wasn't afraid
as he wafted them

wildly away
with shaking,
nail-bitten fingers.

And now the wasps
have invaded again,
building a nest

in the roof-space,
scratching at the eaves
with fierce little jaws,

finding a way into rooms
through closed doors
and windows,

as they did in that other
heat-struck autumn
when we had to lift him

to change the sheets,
or rub surgical spirit
into his heels

and buttocks;
when a dozy wasp
crawled in

under his pyjama top
and clung like a brooch
to his bubbling chest.

THE SINGING TEACHER

'Some girls' voices,' she said
through tight vermilion lips,
'come out like strings of sausages –
yours will have to be worked for.'
I looked down on hennaed hair,
child-size built-up shoes.
Something had gone wrong with her spine
to curl her back like a shrimp's.
I baked her cakes,
brought her bunches of flowers.
Aa-eh-ii-oh-oo, I sang,
while her fat white dog
trembled and whimpered in its dream
and she pinched me with pointed nails.
Oh, Miss Cree, forgive me
for what twisted through you
like a corkscrew: my budding
and growing, my nipples
that stood out like press-studs.

WOMEN'S BLOOD

Burn the soiled ones in the boiler,
my mother told me, showing me how to hook
the loops of gauze-covered wadding pads
onto an elastic belt, remembering
how my grandmother had given her
strips of rag she'd had to wash out
every month for herself: the grandmother
who had her chair by the boiler,
who I loved but was plotting to murder
before she murdered my mother, or my mother –
shaking, sobbing, hurling plates and cups,
screaming she wished she'd never been born,
screeching 'Devil!' and 'Witch!' –
murdered her. I piled up the pads
until the smell satisfied me
it was the smell of a corpse.
'How could you do such a thing?'
my mother asked, finding them
at the bottom of the wardrobe
where the year before she'd found
a cache of navy-blue knickers
stained with the black jelly clots
I thought were my wickedness
oozing out of me.

ROPE

I gripped with my feet, climbed
until I could see through the hoops
of the netball posts; slid back –
burning the skin off my fingers.
Under the mound of coarse new hair,
curved bone, secretly-folded flesh,
where the rope pressed, I'd roused
a live nest: a wriggling litter
like the baby voles I'd found
in a squeaking hole in the grass –
hearts palpitating in furless,
pastry-thin sides; or featherless
chicks – all claws and beaks
and black-veined wings –
that dropped from gutters.
I had to squeeze my thighs
to stop them breaking out –
squealing and squawking
into the gym's blue steel rafters,
or scrabbling down the inside
of my legs, over whitened plimsolls,
making the games mistress shriek.

WHITE FEATHERS

When I still refuse
they put me in the pit:
my feet in water,
sun burning my neck.
I only know the days
by the sky darkening.
When they kill a goose –
throw the feathers in –
I think winter's come.
I'm following my father
up a white field – his gun
cracking and flashing.
It's my job to loop string
round the rabbits' necks
and carry them back –
eyes glazed, legs dangling,
singed holes in their wet fur,
blood like blackcurrant jelly
in the scullery sink.
My father takes the gun up
to my mother's bedroom.
Later, when I clasp my arms
round her waist, press my face
into her petticoat, I smell –
under her rose scent –
the burning whiff
of his hands.

COCKTAILS WITH THE
LEPIDOPTERIST

Wavering, oblivious, his voice unwinds
like the flight of the Blues, Browns,
Gatekeepers, Brimstones

that never stayed still long enough
on my walks over the downs
for me to match the patterns

on their wings with the pictures
in my book; but are laid out
in the drawers of his cabinet

like women abducted from ballrooms
and put to sleep, still wearing
their silken dresses.

'The gentlest way to kill a butterfly
is to leave it in a sealed jar
with a handful of crushed laurel leaves.'

He pours the drinks in a pink-washed
conservatory, pointing out (on the wall
behind him) the Dark Green Fritillary

he mounted – spreading its wings
on a wooden block, pushing
a bright steel pin

through its abdomen,
on the night when upstairs
his wife gave birth to their only child.

RIGHT HAND

Ever since, in an act of reckless
middle-age, I broke my wrist
learning to skate, my right hand

refuses to sleep with me.
It performs the day's tasks
stiffly, stoically; but at night

slides out from the duvet
to hollow a nest in the pillow
like an animal gone to ground

in a hole in the hedge
whose instinct says have nothing
to do with heart, lungs, legs,

the dangerous head. I dreamed of gliding
through a Breughel winter;
of sitting in smoky inns

drinking burning geneva.
My hand dreams its own dream
of escaping: a waving weed rooted

in a pool so icy and numbing
I can feel its ache
rising up my arm.

TEDDY BEARS

After years in the cold
the teddy bears have come back to bed;
brought out of the cupboard under the stairs
like gods completely forgotten
when the times were good.

They're an amiable pair –
a couple of comedians in a silent film,
the sort of companions who don't complain
at losing an eye or an ear,
or having the stuffing knocked out of them.

They are philosophic
about the way life treats them;
even, it seems, about the intruder
who, just as they must have begun to think
they were permanent fixtures,

dislodges them from the pillow
to involve them in a game in which
with noses pressed into the eiderdown
they are 'teddy bears star-gazing',
or, propped dizzily on their heads,

'teddy bears trying to remember something'.
They are souls of discretion.
In the morning we find them
lying on the floor,
blind drunk from politeness.

RUBENS' BOTTOM

You thought it would go on
until the whole house was rubble –
plaster and laths breaking away
in slow motion; a roar like an animal's
released from its cage, or the rage
we used to feel for each other,
my most determined
and unafraid daughter. Then silence,
the air giddy with dust, and you
still standing on the steps
holding the brush above your head,
thinking I'd see it as one more sign
of my whole world collapsing.
You wouldn't let me back
until the debris was shovelled
into builders' sacks, the new plaster
drying, and all I had to worry about
was the colour I'd chosen: a pink
that went on the walls like the pink
of Germolene and rubber sheets.
We bought tubes of burnt sienna
and yellow ochre, stirring
the tints into the paint
with garden sticks, testing
on sheets of newspaper, circling
the tin, crazy now, our arms
moving together like the arms
of witches stirring a broth,
or women in a ritual dance
to deal with loss, until
we arrived at a colour
I, in my rawness, named 'Flesh',
and you, 'Rubens' Bottom'.

LIL'S JIGSAWS

Since Edna got thinner and thinner
and died last winter
Lil's had two passions:
the golden-haired boy next door
and giant jigsaws.

In her front room
three galleons under full canvas
are waiting for her
to mend a splintered sea
before they can slip anchor.

But first, she rubs grass stains
from school cricket whites
with a bar of Vanish
and pegs them out high
on the back yard line

to hang in the sun like angels.
She shuffles to the door
on bunioned feet
and hesitates, as if
when the picture's complete

the hand that grips at her throat
when she climbs the stairs
will pick her out
like a piece of cloud
and fit her into the sky.

FOYLE BRIDGE, DERRY

If I jumped now, holding tight
to clanking carriers
of wine and whiskey,
into what the young chef
on the flight to Belfast
claimed was the fastest flowing
river in Europe, I'd drown.
And even if, on an impulse
to swim and live – leaping free
like a fish from the anger
in and around me – I let them drop
through grey silt water, settling
in a graveyard of prams,
guns, shopping trolleys,
at the muddy bottom,
I'd still drown, sucked
into whirling eddies
that cling like furies
to the plaster-smooth currents
flowing this side of the piers.
I walk past the checkpoint,
past MICKY, SEAMY, PORKY, IRA
scrawled on electric-blue girders.
George, the chef's name was.
He swapped me his seat by the window,
so I'd get a better view
of untouched clouds.

ANTHROPOLOGY

It's like entering the primitive mind:
glass cases crammed full
of collective terrors.
What you come away with at last
isn't the caribou coat you coveted,
or beads for the natives,
or anything useful or valuable,

but only the familiar
and weird: the glossy,
immaculate locks
of the Jivaro enemies'
pickled dolls' heads;
and worse, because you know
(or think you know)

there's nothing curled up
in there, a silver bottle
said to contain a witch
with a label round its neck
promising 'a peck of trouble'
to anyone who's tempted
to draw the stopper.

★

Wanting to shake off
the museum smell – dust,
polish, the sickly-sweet scent
of a grandmother's room
in the weeks she was dying –
you drive in search of unwinding
lanes, drifts of cow-parsley,

a church, a gate, a path over fields
to a stretch of unclouded river:
and find – somewhere between
Kidlington and Kirtlington –
leaning over the ancient packbridge,
looking down where the current
is glassy and swift,

long tendrils of waterweeds
tossing and turning
like restless sleepers
or the waving green hair
of some bewildered old woman
tethered in Cherwell mud
to see if she'll sink or swim.

AT ROISIN'S

We sit in her back yard under a Tree of Heaven,
water trickling round our feet.
She's left the hose running into the pond –
next door are pulling down a wall
and she doesn't want dust to choke the fish.

It was a miracle they survived the winter.
Every morning she had to come out
with buckets of hot water
to melt a hole in the ice
and free them from the frozen weed.

'Let me refresh your glass,' she says,
refilling it to the brim with gin
before I have a chance to protest
and leading me across the crazy paving
to watch the joyously leaping fish.

I used to come here a lot.
It cheered me up – the booze
and her telling me what a fool Bill was
(that I should have smashed a large
irreplaceable vase over his head)

and once a fantastic story
about a woman friend of hers
who hired a private plane
to drop leaflets printed YOU BITCH!
over her husband's mistress's house.

When I got home I'd doze
drunkenly on the sofa,
the children prodding me every so often
as if I was a fish under ice,
testing to see if I was still alive.

FRENCH LESSON

Learning a new language,
you used to tell your pupils
at the night school in Paris,
is to discover another person
you never knew you were.

And now you are teaching me French –
propped up on pillows in bed
because as soon as we stepped off
the cross-channel ferry
you started to shiver with flu.

We begin in a shop.
'Bonjour, Monsieur.' 'Bonjour, Madame.'
'Je m'excuse, je ne parle pas français.'
But how do you say, I ask,
put your arms around me?

Before long we are playing the game
of taking my newly found self
into all the shops in Auffay.
'Embrasse-moi!' I say to the butcher.
'La séduction m'intéresse toujours.'

You are looking flushed.
I wipe your hot face
with a cold wrung-out flannel
and repeat after you:
'Mais d'abord une tasse de thé.'

CLIMBING TINTAGEL

Ghosts don't exist,
you said, except as legends
in our head. But if they did
and we could choose
a haunting place

we wouldn't moon about
in graveyards, or return
to clank around our enemies;
we'd go back to where we once
were happiest: following

Arthur and his queen
up cliff and crag, no longer
stopping to catch breath,
or having to tread carefully
where the path crumbles

and our gaze drops
like a dislodged flint
three hundred feet
to black rocks
and leaping sea;

but leaving loosestrife,
primrose, violet,
untrampled, skimming gorse
and blackthorn hedge –
dancing out over the edge.

STC

for his biographer

First there are the jokes
about how it's going
on the 'South Col'
or the 'Big Sea';
but half-serious,

as if you really had returned
from inching your way
up a vertical rockface,
or sailing single-handed
across his painted ocean.

Then I ask about them –
those friends of yours
I've never met, but you
are now so intimate with
you know the day-to-day state

of souls and bowels.
Is Asra still keeping Sam
on a string? Did he really
see her in bed with William?
How are dear Dorothy's scarlet runners?

I suppose I'm jealous –
as a mountaineer's wife
is jealous of mountains,
or a lone sailor's
of the tug of the sea.

We sit in the Dawn of the Raj
after three days apart,
sharing a Tandoori Mixed Grill,
discussing our passions
and our problems

and you have that far-away look
as if it's all going on
in another room
on another floor
of another century.

THE CRACK

cut right through the house:
a thick wiggly line
you could poke a finger into,
a deep gash seeping
fine black dust.

It didn't appear overnight.
For a long time
it was such a fine line
we went up and down stairs
oblivious to the stresses

that were splitting
our walls and ceilings apart.
And even when it thickened
and darkened, we went on
not seeing, or seeing

but believing the crack
would heal itself,
if dry earth was to blame,
a winter of rain
would seal its edges.

You didn't tell me
that you heard at night
its faint stirrings
like something alive.
And I didn't tell you –

until the crack
had opened so wide
that if we'd moved in our sleep
to reach for each other
we'd have fallen through.

LILY POND

Thinking of new ways to kill you
and bring you back from the dead,
I try drowning you in the lily pond –

holding your head down
until every bubble of breath
is squeezed from your lungs

and the flat leaves and spiky flowers
float over you like a wreath.
I sit on the stones until I'm numb,

until, among reflections of sky,
water-buttercups, spears of iris,
your face rises to the surface –

a face that was always puffy
and pale, so curiously unchanged.
A wind rocks the waxy flowers, curls

the edges of the leaves. Blue dragonflies
appear and vanish like ghosts.
I part the mats of yellow weed

and drag you to the bank, covering
your green algae-stained corpse
with a white sheet. Then, I lift the edge

and climb in underneath –
thumping your chest,
breathing into your mouth.

WHITE TULIPS

Last night I saw you in my dream:
wrenching the hands off clocks,
tearing out springs, weights, jewels.
And now I find you in an orchard,
lying face-up under red blossom
like one of those stone kings
with lion cubs at their feet.
There's a smile on your face;
you're surrounded by white tulips.
You must have cored the earth,
pushed home the papery bulbs
just for this moment – knowing
I'd peer through locked gates,
pressing my forehead against
a blacksmith's tracery
of bells and whorled leaves.
I feel myself shrinking, drying –
skin, bones, nerves, veins
contracting. I fly into the white bowls
of the flowers, emerge sticky with nectar
and pollen, alight on your neck, crawl
under your shirt, and sting.

BITCH SWIMMING

You were the one who acted dog:
imprinting me with a smell
stronger than distance,
disaffection; nose and tongue,
and teeth I could never be sure
were playful, centred on rump
and neck; exciting a bitch
in me, who, while I rehearse
reasons why I'm better off
without you, has leapt
over the wall of a garden,
is in at a door, snuffling
up stairs, pushing her slender
delicate nose into a bed,
whimpering, howling,
tugging at sticky,
stained sheets.
        There's only one way
to lose a scent. I jump into a pool
of unknown depth: surface
among midges, bubbles,
floating feathers –
make us swim for our lives.

JUDITH

Wondering how a good woman can murder
I enter the tent of Holofernes,
holding in one hand his long oiled hair
and in the other, raised above
his sleeping, wine-flushed face,
his falchion with its unsheathed
curved blade. And I feel a rush
of tenderness, a longing
to put down my weapon, to lie
sheltered and safe in a warrior's
fumy sweat, under the emerald stars
of his purple and gold canopy,
to melt like a sweet on his tongue
to nothing. And I remember the glare
of the barley field; my husband
pushing away the sponge I pressed
to his burning head; the stubble
puncturing my feet as I ran,
flinging myself on a body
that was already cooling
and stiffening; and the nights
when I lay on the roof – my emptiness
like the emptiness of a temple
with the doors kicked in; and the mornings
when I rolled in the ash of the fire
just to be touched and dirtied
by something. And I bring my blade
down on his neck – and it's easy
like slicing through fish.
And I bring it down again,
cleaving the bone.

ESTHER

Before the purifying baths,
the anointing with ointments
and oils, the gold robe,
the winding of her crimson
turban, she fills her hands
with dung from the cattle-pen,
goes to the cooks for a knife
wet with lamb's gore. Naked,
kneeling, the black stream
of her unwashed hair flowing
over tiles of blue, red and
green marble, she slashes at locks
that still hold his breath, still
taste of his sweat, are still stiff
with the dried stickiness
of his semen. She mixes a paste
of hair and stinking mud, stuffs
her ears, mouth, the crevice
in her body's soft rock
he turned inside–out
like a purse, the tide
in her rising, spilling over
like boiling mare's milk.

LACRIMAE HOMINIS

You've cried three times, you say:
once when your mother died,
once when you visited her grave,
and now, in powdery dawn,
as I sing, tentatively,
in a breathless, wavering voice,
'The Ballad of Barbara Allen'.
Are you crying? Your eyes shine –
but the cheeks I touch
are hot, waterless.
If I dived into the black light
of your pupils, I'd break my head
in a dry pool. If I took an axe to you,
you'd weep like a fir –
resinous tears, amber drops
hardening in the air.

PARABLE OF THE LETTUCE

I thought he was mad – the vicar –
pulling a long cardboard tube
out of the pulpit, propping it up
on two beach balls we had to imagine
were rocks, and flashing a torch
from the top to illustrate
Seeing the Light. The next week
he held up a lettuce, scattering soil
and drops of water, tearing off
its leaves as if unwrapping
the layers of a mystery parcel,
to prove the existence of God.
And I told him he was mad:
standing up in my dream
in front of the choir boys
and the black-frocked vergers,
my face like the fiery cherubim's.
But now when I picture him –
kneeling among his lettuces
I love him with the love
I feel for all their varieties:
Lamb's, Cos, Spring, Butter,
Webbs, Iceberg, Oak Leaf,
Lollo Rosso, and all the others
whose names I forget. I love him
as I love their greens and reds
and bruised purples; their crisp,
soft, smooth, crinkled, feathery,
curled, round, narrow leaves.
And as I love the creatures
who inhabit their moist interiors:
looping, bright-skinned caterpillars,
snails retreating into coiled corridors,

even the little white grubs
wriggling in the light
like souls in limbo.

STARRY NIGHT

Saint Rémy

A pious town, with a tall steeple
that points to heaven. Behind lit windows
people are laying bread and soup on the tables
and praying: *Dieu soit béni!*
It's a wild night: the stars twirling
in their sockets; cypresses twisting up
out of the red clay like flames.

The doctor's had two calls:
a child struggling to be born –
forcing a passage through rings
of rigid muscle; and a man
with a cancer of the larynx
who's breathing – his wife says –
as if he were running.

It's his friend the schoolmaster.
They spent Wednesday evenings
smoking cherry tobacco and playing chess.
When the doctor's wife ran off
with a violinist, he advised:
'She'll come back if you leave her alone' –
and was proved right.

The girl giving birth
is the dressmaker's daughter.
Seventeen years ago he held her
by the heels, smacked the first cry
out of her throat. He finishes his soup:
a thick broth of barley and carrots.
He's a brave man who doesn't flinch

from using saw or scalpel
on patients tied to his surgery chair.
But there's nothing he can do
to help his old friend out, or ease
the child in, that won't stop their souls
sweeping up in the wind's currents
and swirling past an orange moon.

LATITUDE 65° NORTH

When we were struggling and poor
we dreamed this house:
its bare wood walls, shiny as satin,
the balcony overlooking the fjord
where you'd grow red and white flowers
and I'd write my poems.
We arrived in winter:
had to huddle by the stove
while the wind howled at the door
and the water tossed and frothed
as if the gods were envious.
But now that summer's here
we've carried a table outside;
on all the long light evenings
we sit drinking schnapps
and looking out over the tips of the firs
to a string of islands.
It's all just as we planned.
You sail the boat and fish.
You've planted geraniums and marguerites
all along the edge of the balcony.
I write every day.
We've not seen anyone for weeks.
Tonight I cooked eels
and the golden, horn-shaped chanterelles
I found in the woods this morning
that taste of apricots.
Afterwards you lit a cigar
and refilled our glasses
and we sat in that wonderful,
terrible silence. I'd been reading
a life of Shelley. And I thought:
what if tomorrow a storm blows up?

What if a squall hits your boat?
And I saw myself in a veiled hat
and wearing a long black cloak.
And I tried to remember
the things I used to say
that made you laugh
and pull me onto your knee.
And then you kicked back your stool
and said you'd go crazy.

THE ENGLISH COUPLE AT MESSOPOTAMI

Warmed half by the sun,
half by a stove whose chimney
climbs up, turns a right-angle,
travels across the ceiling
and pokes through a hole
chopped in the window,
they order cutlets, Greek salad,
a jug of the local wine.
There's tinkling of goat bells;
and a black-garbed crone
who watches them eat – grinning,
nodding, smacking her lips,
seeing, even before the chairs
are scraped back from the table,
the twisting donkey path
where he'll climb an olive tree
back into boyhood, while she –
oblivious to the melting snow
that soaks through her coat –
opens to a tongue
moving in waves
like a snake, filling
ears, mouth, every orifice.

SWIMMING IN JANUARY

Because, like every new lover,
I want to enter the underworld
and take you with me, I lead you
into the sea in January – naked into a sea
that flows round our calves and knees
like green fire: deeper and deeper –
feet off the shingle now – gulping half air,
half salt-water, drifting almost to the edge
where there's no returning
before we strike back
to the beach – past windsurfers
sealed in rubber wet-suits, struggling
to lift orange sails, past wading birds
dipping yellow beaks into a film
of mirrored cloud – emerge,
white legs moving like sticks over
oil-blackened sand, at the breakwater
where we draped clothes and towels,
rubbing each other back to life.

is bounding through the forest
with a big smile on his face.
Fruits fall into his hands

from the overhanging branches,
fish leap from streams at his feet.
He thinks he's in paradise.

It's the first day of his holidays.
He's said farewell to his honourable masters,
drained out the tinkling waterclock,

and now he's going to sail his boat
on the lake and write the poems
that all winter have been nibbling

at the lines in his head. But first
he's promised himself he'll mend an old box
with a picture on the lid

cut intricately in jade
of a man bounding through a forest
with a big smile on his face

who keeps a box on his desk
with nothing inside it
to prove that space exists.

AMERICAN NEWSREEL, JAPAN 1945

No one must ever look down on the Son of Heaven.
When the camera-man arrived
with Motsodori in the palace limousine
and found him squatting on the sea-shore
fishing seaweed out of a rockpool
this seemed to pose a problem.

But the living descendant of the Sun Goddess,
whose sky warriors had willingly
dived into enemy ships, and whose premier,
General Hideki Tojo, had taken on his own head
all responsibility for war crimes,
was tired of being a god.

Something he'd learned
in all the hours with his magnifying glass –
researching into sea-snails
as the tide ran out of Segami Bay –
was that one way of surviving
is to be indistinguishable from sand.

THE AVENUE

after Hobbema

This land is so flat
the people who till these fields
still secretly refuse to believe
the world is round.

They plant cabbages and potatoes.
They keep a cow and a pig.
The men carve Meerschaum pipes.
Their women are embroiderers.

On summer evenings they walk out
between tall lines of poplars
brushing midges from their faces
with fat brown hands.

But every fifty years or so
someone tears himself away
from family and farm
and goes in search of the edge.

LOVERS

after Andrew Wyeth

At dawn, he shakes her awake
and gets her to sit on a stool
by the open window.

He studies the way a white
low-lying sun fastens long shadows
down the bank behind the house

and enters the dark room, touching
her cheek, neck, straggling braids,
breast, arm, thigh, ankle.

A dead leaf blows over the sill
and she catches it in her hand,
holds it out like a child.

He orders her to be still,
then sketches it in – the shrivelled leaf
against her live skin.

Her nipples are rosy and hard.
He can smell the fox stink of her sex.
He'll paint her a few more times –

but always buttoned up to the neck
in a heavy loden coat,
further and further from the house,

deeper and deeper
into the frozen woods,
as if returning her to the wild.

VOYAGE

So at last I set a course
for the rough water
beyond the bay;

and all night long –
green and groaning –
I sailed away.

And now, on this calm morning,
I look down into a glassy harbour
where gold- and silver-striped

words are darting,
and the gap-mouthed dead
are floating

and where the flotsam
is so familiar –
things once in my possession

washed there
by a solicitous ocean
to make the landfall welcoming.